EXPLORERS

Marquette and Jolliet

Kristin Petrie

ABDO
Publishing Company

visit us at
www.abdopublishing.com

Published by ABDO Publishing Company, 4940 Viking Drive, Edina, Minnesota 55435.
Copyright © 2007 by Abdo Consulting Group, Inc. International copyrights reserved in all
countries. No part of this book may be reproduced in any form without written permission from
the publisher. The Checkerboard Library™ is a trademark and logo of ABDO Publishing
Company.

Printed in the United States.

Cover Photos: Corbis, North Wind
Interior Photos: Corbis pp. 5, 6, 7, 9, 11, 13, 15; Getty Images p. 21; North Wind pp. 10, 17, 19,
    25, 27, 29

Series Coordinator: Heidi M. Dahmes
Editors: Heidi M. Dahmes, Megan Murphy
Art Direction & Cover Design: Neil Klinepier
Interior Design & Maps: Dave Bullen

Library of Congress Cataloging-in-Publication Data

Petrie, Kristin, 1970-
  Marquette and Jolliet / Kristin Petrie.
     p. cm. -- (Explorers)
  Includes index.
  ISBN-10 1-59679-745-2
  ISBN-13 978-1-59679-745-1
  1. Marquette, Jacques, 1637-1675--Juvenile literature. 2. Joliet, Louis, 1645-1700--Juvenile
literature. 3. Explorers--America--Biography--Juvenile literature. 4. Explorers--France--
Biography--Juvenile literature. 5. Missionaries--Canada--Biography--Juvenile literature. 6.
Canada--Discovery and exploration--Juvenile literature. 7. Canada--History--To 1763 (New
France)--Juvenile literature. 8. Mississippi River--Discovery and exploration--French--Juvenile
literature. I. Title II. Series: Petrie, Kristin, 1970- . Explorers.

F1030.2.P48 2006
977'.01'092341--dc22
                                                                          2005017499

Contents

Explorers

The Mississippi River flows from Minnesota to the Gulf of Mexico. Explorers Jacques Marquette and Louis Jolliet were the first white men to travel the upper Mississippi River.

Native Americans warned Marquette and Jolliet against travel along the Mississippi. According to tall tales, the mysterious river was home to fierce monsters. And, the southern sun would severely burn travelers.

These were pretty good reasons to stay within the boundaries of New France, where both men lived. Nevertheless, Jolliet braved the dangers in the name of exploration. And, Marquette made the courageous journey to spread Christianity.

Marquette and Jolliet introduced Europeans to the Mississippi River. Today, the river is one of North America's most important waterways.

1271
Polo left for Asia

1295
Polo returned to Italy

1254
Marco Polo born

1275
Polo met Kublai Khan

Today, the Mississippi River is one of the busiest commercial waterways in the world!

1460 or 1474
Juan Ponce de León born

1480
Ferdinand Magellan born

1324
Polo died

1475
Vasco Núñez de Balboa born

Young Jacques

Of these two famous explorers, Jacques Marquette was older. Jacques was born on June 1, 1637, in the city of Laon, France. He was the sixth child of Rose de la Salle and Nicolas Marquette. Nicolas was the **seigneur** of Tombelles and the **councillor** of Laon.

At the age of 17, Jacques decided he wanted to be a **Jesuit** priest. So in October 1654, he entered a Jesuit school in Nancy, France. For several years, he studied and worked his way toward becoming a priest.

While at school, Jacques also dreamed of becoming a Roman Catholic **missionary**. Soon, his dream came true. In 1666, Jacques was asked to serve as a missionary

Laon Cathedral

1500
Balboa joined expedition to South America

1493
Ponce de León joined expedition to New World

1502
Ponce de León became governor of Higüey

in New France. This area contained France's new colonies across the Atlantic Ocean in North America.

Before he left, Jacques was **ordained** a **Jesuit** priest. Then, he packed his bags. In June, Jacques boarded a ship at the port of La Rochelle, France. After several weeks crossing the Atlantic Ocean, Jacques arrived in Quebec on September 20, 1666.

At a young age, Jacques knew that he wanted to explore distant lands.

1508
Ponce de León's first expedition

1514
Ponce de León knighted by King Ferdinand II

1513
Ponce de León's second expedition, discovered Florida and the Gulf Stream; Balboa was the first European to sight the Pacific Ocean

Mission Work

Life in Quebec revolved around the fur trade. Trappers went in search of beavers and other animals for their fur. Catholic **missionaries** followed the bold trappers into the wilderness. Their aim was to spread Christianity to Native Americans.

After arriving in Quebec, Marquette spent a year studying Montagnais and other native languages. In time, he would learn up to six Native American languages.

In 1668, Marquette entered the true wilderness. His assignment was to establish a mission among the Ottawa Indians. Marquette assisted in founding Sault Sainte Marie in today's Michigan.

In 1669, Marquette moved again. This time, he traveled to Lake Superior to live among the Huron and the Ottawa. In 1671, the Huron left the mission after a fight with the Sioux. Marquette then founded the Saint Ignace mission on the Straits of Mackinac, in Michigan.

1520
Magellan discovered the Strait of Magellan

1554
Walter Raleigh born

1519
Magellan led expedition to Spice Islands; Balboa died

1521
Ponce de León's third expedition, died in Cuba; Magellan died

In December 1672, a fur trader came to the **mission** with a special invitation. He asked Marquette to join an expedition to the river the Native Americans called the "Messipi." After years of humble service, Marquette's silent prayers to explore were answered.

An Ottawan village

Louis Jolliet

Who was this bearer of great news? His name was Louis Jolliet. Louis was born in 1645, in the settlement of Beaupré, near Quebec. His exact birth date is unknown, but he was **baptized** on September 21.

Louis's parents were Jean Jolliet and Marie d'Abancourt. Jean and Marie had moved to present-day Canada from France when they were children. Jean was a skilled wagonmaker and **wheelwright** for the Company of One Hundred Associates.

The Jolliet family lived near the St. Lawrence River. Louis had an older brother, Adrien, and an older sister, Marie. In time, the children gained a

During his time with the Jesuits, Louis's love of books, music, and drawing flourished.

1580
John Smith born

1585
Raleigh knighted by Queen Elizabeth I

1565
Henry Hudson born

1584–1589
Raleigh sponsored expeditions

younger brother named Zacharie. In 1651, Jean Jolliet died. Marie soon remarried, and the family moved to Quebec.

Louis's formal education began when he was nine or ten. He attended a **Jesuit** college in Quebec. There, Louis showed a special interest in drawing and music. He sketched everything from ships and church symbols to maps.

In 1662, Louis decided to study to become a priest. But by 1667, he had left the Jesuits. His call to adventure and exploration was too strong to suppress.

When he was 13, Louis drew a map of the St. Lawrence River. He declared that one day he would travel the entire river.

Great River

Jolliet traveled for the next few years. He spent a year in France, where historians believe he studied **cartography**. Then, he joined Adrien in the fur business. In summer 1670, Jolliet set out for Sault Sainte Marie to set up a trading post. It was there that he first met Marquette.

While running his trading post, Jolliet often heard stories of a mysterious, great river. Both explorers and Native Americans spoke of this waterway. Today, it is known as the Mississippi River.

The French government was especially interested in this river. They hoped it flowed west to the Pacific Ocean. This would make a swift trade route to the **Far East**.

New France's governor, Louis de Buade, decided to send an expedition to find and chart this river. Buade chose Jolliet and Marquette to lead the expedition. Both men were highly

1595
Raleigh led first expedition

1588
Raleigh helped defeat the Spanish Armada

1606
Smith joined expedition to North America

knowledgeable in Native American languages. And, Jolliet had excellent mapmaking and trading skills.

Jolliet assembled his expedition team in Quebec. Five men, including his younger brother, Zacharie, signed on. Jolliet had one more person left to add to the expedition. So, he traveled to Michigan to find Marquette.

The Mississippi is fondly called the "father of waters" and the "great river."

Planning

On December 8, 1672, Jolliet reached Saint Ignace and Marquette greeted him warmly. Jolliet described the expedition they had been chosen for. Marquette humbly accepted the wonderful opportunity. However, the men needed to wait until spring to begin their journey.

Marquette and Jolliet passed the winter preparing for the upcoming expedition. Jolliet sketched a map of the planned route and surrounding area. The men added rivers that the expedition would need to follow. And, they included place names that they would pass through.

The men also gathered information from Native Americans. They received warnings about the many dangers that awaited them. But, Marquette and Jolliet were not discouraged.

Finally, they gathered equipment and food. Marquette and Jolliet did not know how long their journey would last. But, they were well stocked with corn and smoked meat.

1607
Hudson's first expedition

1609
Hudson's third expedition

1608
Hudson's second expedition

Would You?

Would you know what to pack for a trip if you didn't know how long it would last? How do you think the explorers decided what to bring? What else do you think they packed?

The crew carried equipment that included Jolliet's astrolabe *(right)* and Marquette's traveling altar. Navigators used the astrolabe to calculate time and determine the position of the sun and the stars.

1614
Smith led expedition to North America, charted and named New England

1610-1611
Hudson's last expedition, he died

1616
Raleigh's second expedition

They're Off!

Finally on May 17, 1673, Marquette, Jolliet, and the five **voyageurs** set off from Saint Ignace. The seven men traveled in two birch-bark canoes. They paddled through Lake Michigan, aiming for present-day Green Bay, Wisconsin.

The group covered around 30 miles (48 km) per day. In late May, they reached the Menominee River. Friendly Menominee natives came to the river's edge to greet them. After explaining their assignment, the men received more warnings.

The natives said that the Mississippi River valley was home to man-eating monsters. They claimed the sun would burn the adventurers like firewood. And, the unfriendly peoples along the great river would harm them. But, there was little stopping the explorers. Fearful or not, they continued on.

The expedition left the Menominee village and soon reached Green Bay. There, they entered the Fox River. The expedition followed the Fox River through Wisconsin.

Would you have been brave enough to continue the expedition after hearing the dangers of the Mississippi? How do you think the tall tales were started?

On June 7, Mascouten Indians greeted the travelers. The Mascouten had met French explorers before. So, they were immediately friendly. Marquette and Jolliet's courage impressed the Mascouten. But like the Menominee natives, they feared the great river. Still, two guides joined the expedition to help with the upcoming **portage**.

When the journey continued, Marquette and Jolliet entered territory unknown to Europeans. Eventually, the Fox River came to an end. With the help of the Mascouten guides, the men heaved their canoes on shore.

One and a half miles (2.4 km) of land separated the Fox and the Wisconsin rivers. The portage was difficult. The men trudged through deep mud.

When the explorers reached the Wisconsin River, their native guides turned back. They would not travel any closer to the great river. Marquette prayed for his fellow voyagers. With so many warnings and tall tales, they were all fearful.

1669
La Salle explored Ohio region

1666
La Salle sailed to Canada

1673
Marquette and Jolliet explored the Mississippi River

Marquette and Jolliet were the first Europeans to cross the portage between the Fox and Wisconsin rivers. This important route links the Great Lakes to the Mississippi River.

The Mississippi

On June 17, the expedition reached the Mississippi River. Marquette gave thanks for the group's safety and success. Then the men entered the river. To their surprise, it flowed south. They wondered if the river would turn west and lead them to the Pacific Ocean.

Marquette and Jolliet's team noted many new kinds of wildlife. The men were awed by the enormous buffalo. And, the sturgeon and catfish amazed them. Some of these fish were so large that they nearly knocked the canoes over!

The voyagers paddled two weeks without seeing any signs of human life. Then on June 25, they saw footprints along a muddy shore. So, they stopped their canoes.

Marquette and Jolliet walked about five miles (8 km) inland. They came upon a large Illinois Indian village. Marquette greeted the elders in their language. The natives welcomed the explorers and invited them to feast and rest.

1675
Marquette died

1682
La Salle's second Mississippi River expedition

1679
La Salle's first Mississippi River expedition

Would You?

Would you be able to steer a canoe through raging rapids? Do you think any of the men thought about exploring the Missouri River at a later date?

After several days, the expedition resumed. Travel was uneventful until the men reached the mouth of the Missouri River. **Rapids** and swirling currents made steering difficult. Driftwood and branches threatened to tear their soft birch-bark canoes.

1687
La Salle died

1684
La Salle's third Mississippi River expedition

1700
Jolliet died

Lake Superior

NEW FRANCE

Menominee River

Sault Sainte Marie

Straits of Mackinac

Wisconsin River

Saint Ignace

Minnesota

Wisconsin

Green Bay

De Pere

Fox River

Lake Michigan

Lake Huron

Michigan

Lake Erie

Iowa

Illinois River

Indiana

Ohio River

Illinois

Missouri River

Mississippi River

Missouri

Kentucky

Tennessee

Arkansas

Arkansas River

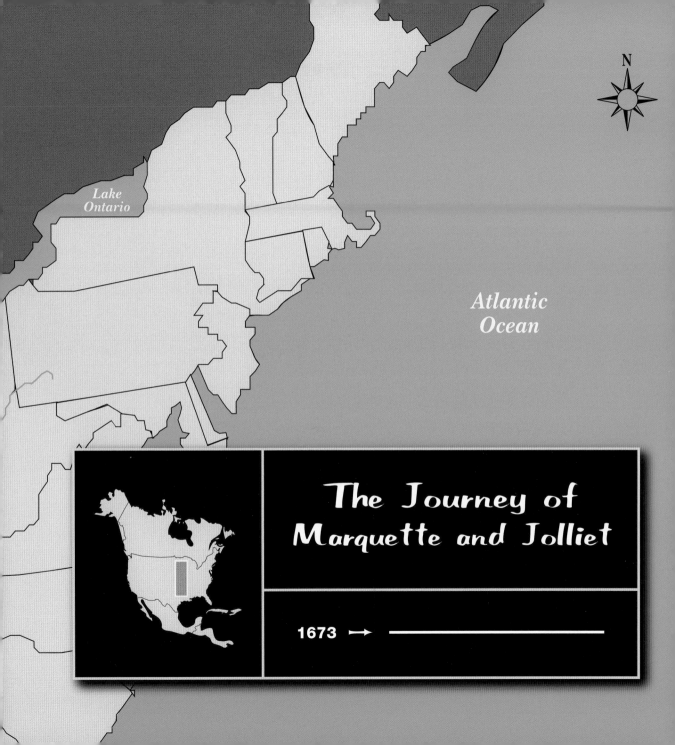

Lake
Ontario

Atlantic
Ocean

N

The Journey of
Marquette and Jolliet

1673 →

More Dangers

On July 16, Marquette and Jolliet neared the mouth of the Arkansas River. There, members of a Quapaw village greeted them in peace.

The explorers cautiously entered the village. They soon learned their location. The natives said the Gulf of Mexico could be reached in just ten days. But again, the leaders received warnings of upcoming dangers. The Quapaw insisted that hostile tribes lived downstream.

Jolliet and Marquette also realized they were nearing Spanish territory. If caught on Spanish land, they would be subject to arrest and even death! The explorers had reached their goal of discovering where the Mississippi led. So, they decided to turn back.

Marquette and Jolliet's expedition turned upstream on July 17. But, paddling against the current was more difficult than expected. They slowly made their way north.

1770
William Clark born

1786
Sacagawea born

1774
Meriwether Lewis born

1800
Sacagawea captured

The explorers left the Mississippi at the Illinois River. The Illinois River brought the explorers to a marshy area near Lake Michigan. From there, the expedition continued north and arrived in Green Bay in late September. There, the men entered the Fox River and headed toward De Pere.

The Arkansas River joins the Mississippi at Desha County, Arkansas.

Final Days

By the time they reached Wisconsin, winter was closing in. Marquette stayed at a **Jesuit mission** in De Pere for the winter months. Historians believe that Jolliet went on to Sault Sainte Marie to check on his fur trade business. He then headed off to Montreal.

Travel was smooth until Jolliet reached the Lachine **Rapids** on the St. Lawrence River. There, his canoe **capsized** while he tried to paddle through the jagged rocks.

Jolliet survived the terrible accident. However his journal, maps, notes, and goods from trading were lost. Jolliet had nothing to show for his expedition.

In October 1674, Marquette decided to return to his mission work. He spent the winter in today's Chicago, Illinois. Marquette became the first European to live there!

Marquette continued his journey in spring 1675. He tried to form a mission near present-day Utica, Illinois. But,

1804
Lewis and Clark began exploring the Pacific Northwest

1806
Lewis and Clark returned to Missouri

1805
Sacagawea joined the Lewis and Clark expedition

**Marquette's writings are the only first-hand
account of their great journey down the Mississippi.**

he became ill with **dysentery**. He needed medical attention,
so he decided to return to Saint Ignace. However, he was too
weak for the journey. Jacques Marquette died May 18, at the
mouth of a river now known as Père Marquette.

1812
Sacagawea died

1856
Robert Edwin Peary born

1809
Lewis died

1838
Clark died

1881
Peary entered the U.S. Navy

Jolliet eventually returned to Quebec. There, he became known as a seal-oil and codfish merchant. In 1675, he married a woman named Claire-Françoise Bissot. The couple later had six children.

Jolliet also continued his work as an explorer and a mapmaker. In 1679, he explored the Hudson Bay. For his service, the French government gave him Anticosti Island in the Gulf of St. Lawrence. He and his family spent their summers on Anticosti and their winters in Quebec.

In his later years, Jolliet explored the Labrador coast and many Canadian rivers. In 1697, he was made royal **hydrographer** of New France. Three years later, Jolliet disappeared while traveling. Louis Jolliet died sometime after May 1700.

Today, Jacques Marquette and Louis Jolliet are honored for their exploration of the upper Mississippi River. They navigated this great waterway from the Wisconsin River to the mouth of the Arkansas River. Their tales of adventure led to further explorations of the Mississippi.

1893
Peary's first expedition

1909
Peary's third expedition, reached the North Pole

1905
Peary's second expedition

1920
Peary died

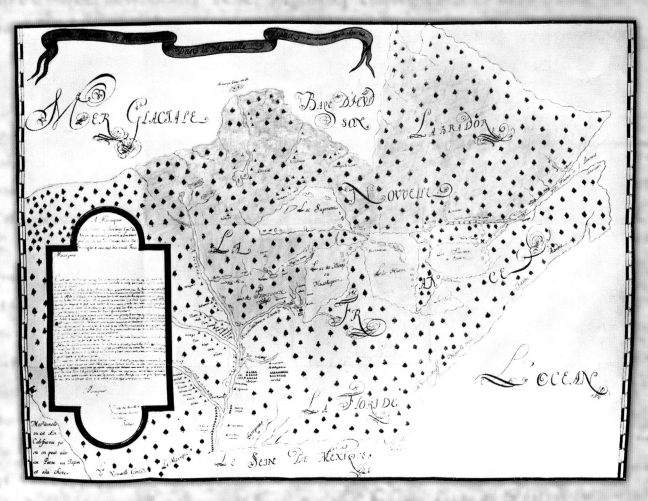

Jolliet lost all of the maps he had made during the
Mississippi expedition. So in 1674, Jolliet drew this map
from memory. It shows how he believed New France looked.

Glossary

baptize - to be admitted into the Christian community during a ceremony involving the ritual use of water.

capsize - to turn over.

cartography - the science or art of mapmaking.

councillor - a member of a group of people who meet to make a decision, give advice, or discuss a problem.

dysentery - a disease of the intestines.

Far East - usually considered to consist of the Asian countries bordering on the Pacific Ocean.

hydrographer - one who charts bodies of water.

Jesuit - a member of the Roman Catholic Society of Jesus, which was founded by Saint Ignatius Loyola in 1534.

mission - a center or headquarters for religious work. A missionary is a person who spreads a church's religion.

ordain - to officially become a minister or a priest.

portage - the transporting of boats or goods across land from one body of water to another.

rapid - a fast-moving part of a river. Rocks or logs often break the surface of the water in this area.

seigneur - a man of rank or authority.

voyageur - a man employed by a fur company to transport goods to and from remote stations.

wheelwright - a maker and repairer of wheels and wheeled vehicles.

Saying It

Beaupré - boh-PRAY
De Pere - dih PIHR
Laon - LAHN
Louis de Buade - lwee duh byoo-awd
Menominee - muh-NAH-muh-nee
Sault Sainte Marie - soo saynt muh-REE
seigneur - sayn-YUHR
voyageur - voy-uh-ZHUHR

Web Sites

To learn more about Jacques Marquette and Louis Jolliet, visit ABDO
Publishing Company on the World Wide Web at **www.abdopublishing.com**.
Web sites about Marquette and Jolliet are featured on our Book Links page.
These links are routinely monitored and updated to provide the most current
information available.

Index